Baseline Assessment, Curriculum and Target Setting

for Pupils with Profound and Multiple Learning Difficulties

Sonia Maskell
and Fran Watkins

with Elizabeth Haworth

Edited by Erica Brown

David Fulton Publishers
London

David Fulton Publishers Ltd
Ormond House, 26–27 Boswell Street, London WC1N 3JZ

www.fultonpublishers.co.uk

First Published in Great Britain by David Fulton Publishers 2001

Note: The right of the Sonia Maskell, Fran Watkins, Elizabeth Hayworth and
Erica Brown to be identified as the authors/editors of this work has been asserted
by them in accordance with the Copyright, Designs and Patents Act 1988.

British Library Cataloguing in Publication Data
A catalogue record for this book is available from the British Library

ISBN 1–85346–690–5

The publishers would like to thank Christine Avery for copy-editing and Sheila Harding
for proofreading this book.

Typeset by Mark Heslington, Scarborough, North Yorkshire
Printed in Great Britain by Bell and Bain Ltd, Glasgow

Contents

Introduction

This book sets out to help teachers and other professionals who are involved in assessment and target setting for pupils whose complex learning difficulties place them at the earliest levels of development. It aims to serve as a valuable tool to specialist teachers of pupils with a wide range of profound and complex needs, and offers educationalists with less experience of Profound, Multiple and Complex Learning Difficulties a comprehensive and easy to follow guide, in the assessment and target setting process.

Readership

The book is based on the premise of the authors that a balance between delivery of small-steps, skill-based individual learning objectives and wider learning opportunities is crucial to the holistic development of the child. Throughout the book readers are offered a logical, structured, developmental framework and shown ways of ensuring a breadth of experiential learning opportunities through schemes of work, designed to complement ongoing skill-based assessments.

In the book the authors refer to these children as having Profound and Multiple Learning Difficulties (PMLD).

The Baseline Assessment and Target Setting Assessment Scheme (BATS) is an holistic approach to the education provision for pupils with PMLD. It has been written, trialled, implemented, revised and developed by specialists at Mordaunt School, Southampton in discussion with a range of professionals, consultants and experienced teachers of SEN. Development of the scheme started in 1994 and the scheme has been used in the school for over six years. It has proved to be very successful in individual assessment and group target setting for pupils who have particular education needs and who are at the extreme boundaries of the special needs continuum. Those involved in its compilation recognised that guidance and assessment material for teachers of pupils with

Background

PMLD was lacking in certain areas. Areas included planning, target setting, curriculum delivery, records, recording of progress monitoring schedules and schemes of work. This book discusses each of these areas of provision and offers – throughout Part Two and in the Appendix – a range of documentary examples and exemplification materials which can be photocopied or adapted for use with pupils with PMLD and those with other complex learning difficulties.

Acknowledgements

We would like to extend our special thanks to the following people without whom the book would not have been possible:

David Fulton and his team for presenting us with the prestigious Fifth Fulton Fellowship Award in Special Education at Westminster Institute of Education, Oxford.

All the staff at Mordaunt School Southampton and particularly the pupils who provided the inspiration and motivation for our work.

The Rose Road Association for their continued support.

Our families and partners for their patience, support and understanding throughout the writing phase; and particular thanks to Clive Watkins for his ICT skills.

Erica Brown, our editor, formerly Head of Special Education at Westminster Institute of Education, Oxford and now Head of Research and Development at Acorns Children's Hospice Trust in Birmingham.

Part One

The Rationale

The authors in consultation with the whole school staff were able to define a series of important principles which they considered underpinned the philosophy of their work and which linked to all the documentation which subsequently developed. A statement of these principles is as follows:

Philosophy

- Every pupil has a fundamental right to be able to communicate.
- Every pupil has the right to develop his or her ability to communicate, at whatever level, and to be given the opportunity to respond to and control his or her environment.
- Every pupil should be enabled to access all channels of communication at every opportunity for effective communication.
- Every pupil should be given time to make his or her own individual response.
- Every pupil has the right to be positioned correctly and comfortably in order for learning to take place.
- Every pupil has the right to be treated with dignity, courtesy and privacy and due regard should be given to his or her wishes where appropriate.
- Every pupil should be encouraged to achieve a level of independence through graduated stages, however small these stages may be. Relevant and appropriate praise and reward and the celebration of achievement play a vital role in the successful learning process.
- Every pupil has the right to an effective partnership between home and school.

- Every pupil has the right to a supportive caring atmosphere that promotes success and acknowledges that we can learn from our mistakes.
- Every pupil has the right to age-appropriate activities, bearing in mind that within any learning situation it is necessary to have due regard to the developmental level of each pupil.
- Every pupil has the right to equality of opportunity.

It is interesting to note that while we were working on developing our policy and implementing our practice other practitioners were developing similar ideas. Our philosophy with regard to the importance of communication links closely with that of Ware (1996) when she describes a particular type of interactive environment which she calls a 'responsive environment'.

According to Ware responsive environments are important to pupils with PMLD because:

- they are positive environments to be in (for both pupils and staff)
- they capitalise on individual strengths such as differences in approach, tone of voice between staff members and the different relationships that develop between staff and pupils
- they can help pupils with PMLD to make progress.

Towards a definition for PMLD

The Warnock Report (DES 1978) recommended the abolition of categorisation of handicap. Alternative categories for SEN were introduced, including Severe Learning Difficulties (SLD), Emotional and Behavioural Difficulties (EBD) and Physical Disabilities (PD). Despite a statement in the SCAA document *Planning the Curriculum* (1996b) which says that pupils at the extreme boundaries of the SEN continuum 'are not a homogeneous group', the term Profound and Multiple Learning Difficulties has become the increasingly accepted terminology to describe those pupils functioning at the earliest levels of development and at the extreme boundary of the SEN continuum. It is therefore understandable that there is a wide variance in the definition of Profound and Multiple or Complex Learning Difficulties both nationally and individually. Ware and Healey (1994) define PMLD as 'having two or more severe impairments, one of which is profound learning difficulties', while another widely accepted definition contained in the SCAA document (1996b) states that pupils with PMLD:

> *. . . appear to be functioning at the earliest levels of development and [who], additionally, have physical or sensory impairment. Some of these pupils may be ambulant and may also behave in ways that either challenge staff and other pupils or result in their isolation making it difficult to involve them positively in educational experiences. Most experience difficulties with communication.*

Although there is much to commend in this definition, the authors consider that all pupils with PMLD will experience difficulties with communication and they would challenge the suggestion that some pupils may be ambulant. Ware (1996) pointed out that the term 'profound and multiple learning difficulties' was a description of the degree of someone's learning difficulties. She suggested that this term referred to someone functioning at a developmental level below the age of two years and frequently under one year whilst also having one or more disabilities. In light of the significant levels of disability of all pupils in the school in which the BATS document was developed, the authors suggest a definition should state that *all* pupils with PMLD have the sort of learning difficulty embraced in the description from Ware. Additionally they may have a physical disability together with actual or perceptual sensory impairment. The authors would argue that pupils with PMLD are likely to have additional medical difficulties, such as the need for enteral feeding, seizures or acute breathing and chest problems.

Historical background and context of special education

The 1944 Education Act made reference to the 'Special Educational Treatment' (SET) of some children and stipulated certain categories of 'handicap' requiring educational provision according to 'age, aptitude and ability'. This in turn influenced the development of segregated educational provision, thus increasing the number and range of training centres. However, it was not until the 1970 Education (Handicapped Children) Act that for the first time it was acknowledged that all children, regardless of disability, have the right to receive an education. The Act emphasised that educational access must be the right of *all* children, including the formerly excluded group of pupils who had a wide range of needs, and who functioned at the very earliest levels of development. Prior to this legislation, one group of children had remained the responsibility of the health authorities and were labelled as 'Educationally Sub-normal'.

The Warnock Report (DES 1978) laid the foundations for the legislation contained in the Education Act of 1981 and helped to pave the way for the continuing changes and reform in all areas of Special Educational Provision. Improvement in assessment procedures, a strengthening of parental rights, a tightening up of procedural processes and a bid to strengthen the partnership between education, health and social service were some of the important issues that the government attempted to address during the period of change. The Report further advocated that use of the word 'handicap' be removed and recommended the abolition of categories of handicap, which should be replaced with the term 'Special Educational Needs'. It was also from this point that all children were placed on a 'continuum of special needs' which proved to be the catalyst that transformed the principles and practice of SEN assessment. Parents started to put increasing pressure on the judicial system in order to acquire the special or mainstream school placement they favoured. Procedures were set up to identify the special educational needs of children which required a formal, multidisciplinary assessment.

Special educational provision was also greatly affected by the 1988 Education Reform Act, which included significant reform of the entire educational system as well as increasing the rights of parents whilst effectively reducing the substantial powers of Local Educational Authorities (LEAs). It was the 1988 Education Reform Act which continued to strengthen the move towards far-reaching changes to the assessment procedure with the introduction of a national assessment framework, *The Code of Practice on the Identification and Assessment of Special Educational Needs* (DfE 1994).

The 1993 Education Act together with the Code of Practice (DfE 1994) attempted to clarify the roles and responsibilities of both the school and the LEAs with regard to pupils with SEN. Much of the emphasis was placed on ensuring that a structured and appropriate assessment was carried out. As a result, a series of recommendations which related to the implementation process of the Code of Practice were drawn up and these are outlined below.

- All children with SEN should be identified as early and as quickly as possible.
- Provision for children with SEN should be made by the most appropriate authority.
- Where needed the LEA must make assessments and

statements in accordance with time limits, must write clear and thorough statements and carry out annual reviews of provision.

- The wishes of the child should be taken into account and considered in light of his or her maturity and understanding.
- There must be close cooperation with all agencies concerned and a multidisciplinary approach must be used.

Ensuring that all pupils, including those with PMLD, have access to a broad and balanced curriculum relevant to their individual needs is an ongoing challenge which requires regular review of curriculum content, teaching approaches, management of the classroom, equipment and support staff and criteria for the planning and delivery of lessons. The introduction of the National Curriculum which resulted from the Education Reform Act of 1988 was the catalyst that helped teachers to significantly broaden a curriculum that had become increasingly narrow, in many special schools, because of an over-emphasis on the development of communication and independence skills (Sebba *et al.* 1993). However it soon became evident that instead of supplementing individual skill-based learning, an adapted National Curriculum was favoured by many schools and some special schools lost their direction. A number of LEAs and educational working parties independently started to draft a series of curriculum documents, such as Hampshire County Councils' *Working Within Level One of the National Curriculum* (1993); Northern Ireland Curriculum Council's *Stepping Stones* (1991) and Kent Curriculum Services Agency's *Crossing the Bridge* (1995) and *Crossing the Bridge II* (1996). These curriculum documents were generally designed to aid special schools in their quest to provide an appropriate curriculum for pupils with Severe and Profound Learning Difficulties. There was, however, little effective interchange of ideas between practitioners and, although some good practice developed, special schools often felt isolated. Some schools developed curriculum and assessment materials appropriate to their pupils, but this state of affairs contributed to a lack of consistency in curriculum delivery and assessment materials.

Statutory requirements and recent changes in the law

The government's Green Paper *Excellence For All Children: Meeting Special Educational Needs* (DfEE 1997) is arguably the most far-reaching national review of SEN provision since Mary Warnock published her revolutionary report in 1978. Very soon after the new government's election to office, it was evident that a fundamental appraisal of the entire current educational system was underway, from preschool to further and higher education. Life-long learning opportunities were proposed. Not only did policies speak of excellence, collaboration, inclusion and partnership, but they were also the catalyst for a climate where improving educational standards was seen to be of paramount importance. A call was made for a process of national planning and regional development to encourage skills enhancement, sharing of specialist expertise, research opportunities, performance tables, school improvement and across the board target setting.

In the document *Meeting Special Educational Needs – A Programme For Action* (DfEE 1998) the government produced a programme for action that sets out the framework for responding to special education provision up to 2002. In addition, a review of the National Curriculum was instigated in order to develop the school curriculum further and, in an attempt to be 'responsive to changes in society and the economy and changes in the nature of schooling itself' (QCA and DFEE 1999). As a result, Curriculum 2000 was developed and by 2002 this should be fully implemented in schools.

Baseline assessment

The need for an accurate and rigorous baseline assessment upon which the building blocks of future learning are founded has been increasingly identified as an important starting point for all pupils. It became a statutory requirement in September 1998. Baseline assessment can be seen as a multi-faceted tool which will help to ascertain a child's abilities, link the information with future skill-based objectives, assist in target setting and identify future learning needs. Additionally strengths and weaknesses are highlighted and these assist in the early identification of SEN, which can inform teaching strategies and early intervention programmes for children with learning difficulties. Furthermore it becomes an instrument to measure and monitor pupil progress.

In addition to these child-centred purposes and values of a baseline assessment, there are also a number of school foci including accountability and value-added elements. These elements act as a tool in resource planning and serve as positive influences in the budget projection in school improvement.

From September 1998 all maintained schools are required to use an accredited Baseline Assessment Scheme. These assessments are to be designed appropriately for children who started primary school before the required compulsory age of entry. Therefore they need to be linked with the *Desirable Outcomes for Children's Learning on Entering Compulsory Education* (SCAA 1996a) which was superseded by the *Early Learning Goals: Curriculum Guidance for Foundation Stage* (SCAA 2000) in September 2000.

The baseline assessment can be a measure of an individual pupil's progress throughout his/her own school career and also be used as a benchmark against other groups of pupils both locally and nationally (DfEE 1997). It closely resembles the accountability elements in the Statutory Assessment Tests (SATs) at the end of each Key Stage.

P levels

In 1998 QCA commissioned the National Foundation for Educational Research (NFER) to produce the first draft of criteria for P levels through consolidating the best elements of the range of widely used assessment schemes available to teachers of pupils with SEN. This draft was revised after initial consultation and became known as *Supporting the Target Setting Process* (QCA 1998). The performance criteria are now known as P levels. The criteria were developed to support schools by providing a common basis for measuring the progress of pupils for whom the early levels of the National Curriculum are not appropriate. P levels are intended to provide a framework against which the progress of pupils can be measured using the school's own assessment scheme. Attainment can be mapped. The first three descriptions are the same in each scale as they describe early development which is common across areas of the curriculum. This premise links in with the belief of Mordaunt School concerning commonality of early stages of development across the curriculum, and is expanded in Part Two under Records of attainment.

Data on pupil attainment is collected by the school in order to set a baseline from which whole-school targets can be identified, as part of the annual cycle of school improvement. There are three scales of performance criteria in each of Language and Literacy, Mathematics, and Personal and Social Development. Each of the scales in Language and Literacy and Mathematics contains eight descriptions from P1 to P8.

If the majority of pupils are operating between P1 and P3 and where the descriptions of attainment are generic and do not show subject differentiation (as in P4 to P8) then targets for whole-school improvement cannot be based on different subject areas. However, because of the unique nature of pupils with PMLD, setting individual targets and aggregating these goals is one of the ways of showing whole-school improvement. Learning for these pupils takes place in such small steps that predicting progress within the P levels is likely to prove unreliable since these steps are too broad.

Male (2000) states that:

> *Progress is likely to be conceptualised and evidenced quite differently for pupils with degenerative and/or life threatening conditions who now constitute up to 10 per cent of the SLD school population . . . progress may at best be evidenced by the maintenance of skills, knowledge and awareness while for others it may mean the minimising of regression.*

Within our own school we have seen the evidence of pupils maintaining skills through their identified learning objectives as well as pupils with degenerative conditions (such as Retts Syndrome) showing regression due to the inherent nature of their condition. In pupils with life threatening conditions their severe health problems can cause regression in times of crisis.

Progress for our pupils with PMLD does not necessarily mean a steady increase in the acquisition of skills, but may be a roller-coaster of gain, maintain and loss. This is why we believe that providing learning opportunities is such an important and valid way of measuring progress in pupils with PMLD, allowing them to experience what Male (2000) refers to as 'a greater willingness to experience, and a broadening of skills, knowledge and awareness'.

School profile

The school in which the Baseline and Target Setting document was developed is an independent special day school run by a voluntary organisation which is actively supported by its local City and County Councils. It is an example of the positive partnership between the voluntary sector and local authorities that has increasingly been promoted in the government's Green Paper (DfEE 1997) *Excellence For All Children: Meeting Special Educational Needs*. Pupils at this small, co-educational special school are aged between two and 19 years, and all have profound and multiple learning difficulties.

The school is housed in purpose-built premises in a residential area of north Southampton and seeks to offer the highest possible standards of education and therapy within a stimulating environment. Facilities include a therapy room, multi-sensory and soft play rooms, a hydrotherapy pool and sensory gardens, all of which help staff and pupils to explore a variety of new and different experiences. The school provides access to a broad, balanced, relevant and differentiated curriculum, which addresses all curriculum areas within the National Curriculum. This is balanced with individual learning objectives and the range of assessment materials used by the school have been compiled into the BATS document.

Building strong and positive partnership links is considered a vital part of all initial pupil referrals and all 'new' parents and carers have a home visit where they complete a profile of their son or daughter with the Early Years teacher. The school enjoys an 'open door' policy and parents and carers are encouraged to spend time in their child's new class with the school staff. Home visits are frequently arranged (either in term time or during the school holidays) as a result of each child's annual review and may involve the teacher and other school staff, such as the occupational therapist, the school nurse, the speech and language therapist or the physiotherapist.

The school has always recognised that discussion and information sharing between teaching and other school staff and the home is essential, and parents and carers are encouraged to act as partners in the education of their children. Developing regular, appropriate and two-way communication systems between the school and home is regarded by the authors as a key to success in the ongoing assessment and review process that spans a pupils entire life at school. We welcomed the implementation of the DfEE *Home School Agreements* Framework (1998a).

The Annual Review and Transition Plans are regarded by the authors as a vitally important part of the ongoing assessment process where individual needs are reviewed and targets reassessed. Although the authors consider that review and assessment of individual programmes should be an ongoing process, the annual overview is an opportunity for a focused interdisciplinary assessment giving an opportunity for parents and carers to meet with their child's teacher, therapists and any other relevant professionals to discuss progress, set future objectives and review any changes in educational or non-educational provision. The assessment and target setting BATS document embraces all subject areas of the National Curriculum as detailed below.

English

As communication is of prime importance and a vital part of daily life, it is given a high priority within the English curriculum. Communication is about expressing needs and desires and therefore provides the ability to control the environment. It is also about understanding and sharing the real and imagined world and gives meaning to events and situations. Hence, we believe that the development of all communication skills, especially non-verbal and augmented communication for our pupils who have limited or no use of speech, is a crucial aspect of their education.

Mathematics

Mathematics is an integral part of everyday life and is an essential component of the learning process. For those pupils in the early stages of cognitive development mathematics should be practical and relevant in order to develop awareness and understanding of their world.

Science

Science provides a variety of experiences for all pupils in order to develop their ability to reach out, explore and investigate the world through their senses. The sensory curriculum plays an important part in science through giving opportunities to experience and develop taste, smell, touch, vision, sound and bodily sensations.

Art

Art is a means of exploring, organising and expressing an understanding of the world as well as personal experiences in an imaginative and creative way. It provides opportunities for creative ability and encourages the exploration of different media as well as developing visual and tactile skills enabling the fullest involvement in and the appreciation of artistic experiences.

Technology

Technology is concerned with the acquisition of manual skills and problem solving. Pupils learn from the real world about them and therefore the steps of problem solving are embedded in the learning contexts which are familiar and natural to them.

Geography

Geography is mainly concerned with pupils developing an interest in and extending their awareness of their surroundings. Geography provides a variety of experiences and opportunities for all pupils to react and interact with people in their own community and to develop an interest in people and places beyond their immediate experience.

History

History is concerned with pupils developing an understanding of regular patterns in time, of continuity and change over time, of cause and effect in terms of social actions, and with the development of their interest and understanding of their past.

Music

Music is a life-enriching experience for all members of society. Music plays a major role in daily life and is a prominent and powerful means of communication and expression. Musical experiences give opportunities for the development of more general and transferable skills. Music is also an important vehicle for developing and improving self-awareness, self-esteem and confidence.

Physical education

Movement experiences are fundamental to the development of all pupils and are particularly important to pupils with special needs who often have difficulty in relating to their own bodies and to other people. Emphasis is on developing general skills relating to the mastery of many aspects of movement that can be applied to different physical tasks, rather than particular skills for certain sports or activities.

The PE curriculum provides for pupils' increasing self-confidence in their ability to manage themselves and their bodies within a variety of movement situations. PE serves to enable pupils to experience success, a sense of achievement and an awareness of self-worth. PE embraces all areas of physical mobility including physiotherapy and horse-riding as well as basic movement skills, swimming and outdoor and adventurous activities.

Personal, social and health education/citizenship

Personal, social and health education is an explicit part of the school's curriculum and takes place across the pupils' whole learning experience. Its success depends on the ethos of the school and is therefore encompassed within the school's core values. Sex education is an integral part of PSHE and is delivered when appropriate to individual pupils.

Information and communication technology

ICT is an element of the curriculum crucial to our pupils. It can enhance the ability of pupils to communicate and provides opportunities for all to develop choice and control.

Modern foreign languages

Modern foreign languages provide pupils with meaningful opportunities to experience languages, cultures and traditions which are not their own. The programme is covered in blocks of time rather than as an ongoing subject.

In addition to the National Curriculum the following areas play an important part in the pupils' learning experience:

- **Religious education** In RE there is knowledge to be learned and there are skills to be developed; there are attitudes to be encouraged and emotions to be explored; there is self-understanding to be nurtured and developed and an identity to be fashioned; there are personal beliefs to be formed.
- **Collective worship** It is important to recognise the guidance in the 1988 Education Reform Act which states that collective worship should be 'wholly or mainly of a broadly Christian character'. The main emphasis in school worship follows the traditions of Christian belief while recognising the faiths and cultures represented by all pupils in the school.

All subjects are likely to be taught in a cross-curricular way. However, in any lesson there will be a main subject focus.

Acquisition of communication skills within a responsive environment

As stated in our philosophy, the environment of the pupil with PMLD plays a crucial part in the acquisition of communication skills. Research by Houghton *et al.* (1987) and Hanzlik (1990) on early infant interaction with adults shows that long before the infant has any intent to communicate adults treat the baby as though actions have meaning. The evidence suggests that it is through this that the baby learns to communicate (Scoville 1984).

Houghton *et al.* (1987) state that non-disabled pupils at the same developmental age are active participants in interactions with their primary carers and this active participation is regarded as important for their development. By contrast pupils with severe disabilities received only a very few responses to their initiations. Hanzlik (1990) believed that mothers of infants with developmental delay were more directive and less positive in their interactions than mothers of non-disabled infants. Further research by Terdal *et al.* (1976) and Cunningham *et al.* (1981) has provided evidence that parents find it more difficult to respond to children with disabilities than to non-disabled children. They are more likely to experience negative or unsatisfying interactions with them so that infants with disabilities of all kinds are less likely to experience a responsive environment than non-disabled infants.

In creating a responsive environment we need to take into account factors that could affect the acquisition of communication skills. Ware (1996) states that pupils with PMLD may not vocalise as frequently as the non-disabled child. They may have more unconventional communication behaviours such as tongue thrusts, eye blinks and changes of position. Furthermore they may produce very few behaviours, with long pauses in between, so it is difficult for the other person to get a feel for the rhythm of their communication; or there may be very little rhythm and interaction.

Through experiences and research at our school we have come to the same conclusions as Ware that the necessary components of creating a responsive environment include:

- Responding to the actions of the child, i.e. waiting for the pupil to respond. A pupil with PMLD may respond very slowly, not at all, or in an unexpected way.
- Having an expectation that a pupil will respond, for example by the adult looking attentively at the pupil. This increases the likelihood of interaction.
- Individual children taking the lead in interactions through turn-taking as discussed by Nind and Hewett (1994). This may be facilitated by waiting for the child to act first, imitating the child's behaviour and following the child's lead, a process known as Intensive Interaction.

The end result of a responsive environment for a pupil with PMLD is that through continual opportunities for interaction, the pupil is seen as a communicator and therefore learns to communicate. All our pupils are communicators, whether intentionally or pre-intentionally. In attempting to define pre-intentional communication we use Goldbart's (1994) definition: '. . . information that teachers can decode from the behaviour of pupils not yet sending messages'(p. 16).

Holistic, interdisciplinary assessment

An holistic approach to education provision for pupils with PMLD and other complex needs is of great importance and includes multidisciplinary collaboration in the assessment process. This is vitally important and it is a statutory requirement laid down in the Children Act 1989. In assessing and delivering a single educational objective (i.e. in the area of communication), the needs of a child who is functioning at the earliest levels of development are similar across a range of professional contexts. For example, the teacher and the speech and language therapist need to liaise in order to assess where an individual child is in terms of his/her own development. The physiotherapist needs to be consulted to ensure that positioning is appropriate and the occupational therapist (in conjunction with the teacher) may need to assess the child for hand splints and communication equipment such as switches. Furthermore, the medical team and the teacher might liaise about medical regimes and enteral feeding. Thus there are a considerable number of professionals involved in assessing and delivering a single objective and the teacher is central to this process.

Pupil assessment must be seen as an ongoing and seamless process, which links assessment with the identification of a pupil's educational needs and learning objectives. This should span a child's life at school and should not be regarded as a series of unrelated snapshot sessions which occur at various points throughout a pupil's life. Rather, assessment is an ongoing and interrelated framework which feeds into a pupil's individual target setting.

According to Ware and Healey (1994) there are three main issues to be taken into consideration when deciding which type of assessment will be most suitable. First, it must be ascertained what will be measured to demonstrate progress. Second, the instrument used to measure progress should be chosen. Third, the relevance or usefulness of the assessment in informing teaching should be considered.

Systems of assessment that have most commonly been used for pupils with PMLD include the Uzgiris and Hunt Scales of Sensorimotor Development (Uzgiris and Hunt 1975); *Behaviour Assessment Battery* (Kiernan and Jones 1982); *Pre-Verbal Communication Schedule* (Kiernan and Reid 1986); Assessment and Management of Children with Multiple Handicaps (Simon 1986); the Initial Profile Checklist (Ouvry 1987). Assessments in use at the present time include *Vision for Doing* (Aitkin and Buultjens 1992); *Early Steps Summative Assessment* (Byrom 1999), all of which, in their own way, are valuable tools. At Mordaunt School we considered these models but chose to continue to use the Hampshire County Councils' *Working Within Level One* General Skills section of maths, English and science because the framework started at a level that was early enough to be appropriate to all our pupils. We were able to adapt it to form the basis of our Records of Attainment, recording skills from their emergence to consolidation. We were aware of gaps and the possibility that graduated steps within the assessment might have been 'in the wrong order'.

If an assessment begins at an early enough level, and there are enough pointers within it, a teacher should have enough information to write a relevant Individual Learning Programme (a small-skill-based objective) appropriate to individual needs. Furthermore, there may be occasions when a teacher refers to other assessment tools or uses these to inform target setting.

In Part Two we describe how the staff of Mordaunt School produced their own Baseline Assessment and Target Setting document and the Mordaunt School curriculum, both of which enable their pupils with PLMD to receive an appropriate inclusive education. When reference is made to 'we', this refers to the school senior management team, the teaching staff and the special school assistants, all of whom were involved in a process of consultation. Names of pupils have been changed to protect their identity.

Part Two

The Process

We recognised that baseline assessment was going to become a statutory requirement but we did not want a framework imposed upon us which might not be entirely appropriate to our students. We were also concerned about the consultation document, *National Standards for Special Educational Needs (SEN) Specialist Teachers* (Teacher Training Agency 1998), because one of the nine draft standards had amalgamated SLD and PMLD into the category Severe and Profound Learning Difficulties (SLD). When looking in detail at this category in both the Knowledge and Understanding and the Skills sections, we felt the skills of the teacher necessary to meet the needs of pupils with PMLD were not adequately covered. Other standards, particularly deaf/blindness, physical disabilities, speech language and communication difficulties and visual impairment detailed the skills necessary to meet the needs of pupils with PMLD more comprehensively. We were anxious that the category of PMLD would be lost and therefore the skill and expertise of the specialist teacher of pupils with PMLD would at the very least be marginalised, or at worst, go unrecognised.	*Principles*

We are aware that the definition of PMLD means that all our students will have specific individual needs, and an 'off the shelf' available assessment would not be suitable. A group of head teachers from the Hampshire Consortium of SLD schools had also seen the need for a baseline assessment to suit their requirements, so a working party was set up to address this issue. From this working party a draft baseline assessment framework was developed and was to be trialled over a period of a year within the member schools. However, because of various circumstances (LEA reorganisation, possible accreditation for Life and Living Skills Scheme etc.) the other member schools did not proceed. Mordaunt School decided it could be a useful basis for our own document.

The resulting baseline assessment was one link in the chain of our holistic approach to the education of our pupils. In order to produce the whole we needed to put all these links together in one document called Baseline Assessment and Target Setting. Most of the scheme has been developed, trialled, implemented, revised and has been in use in Mordaunt School since 1996. The assessment scheme is a practical guide to enable specialist teachers of pupils with PMLD to achieve the correct balance between small-step skill-based learning objectives delivered through an individual learning programme and a range of experiences from the PMLD curriculum delivered through experiential schemes of work at the level appropriate to each individual pupil.

Once baseline assessment became a statutory requirement it was apparent to us that all our other documentation needed to be gathered together to show the interrelated nature of this holistic approach. Thus BATS became our assessment scheme. It should not be regarded as a series of unrelated sections but a carefully structured and interrelated framework, where assessment feeds into individual target setting. Thus we looked in detail at the following documentation.

- Initial assessment – This is Me
- Individual learning programmes (ILP)
- Records of attainment
- Curriculum (Mordaunt School)
- Schemes of work
- Eating and drinking – including enteral feeding
- Moving and handling.

Individual education plans

At this point it may be necessary to elaborate, to help you to understand our terminology. By IEP we mean an Individual Education Plan which is a working file containing all the information about a student to enable him or her to access the whole educational process. This file could contain all or some of the elements in Figure 2. We would recommend that all items with an asterisk should always be included in an IEP. In our experience all of the elements in Figure 2 contribute to a comprehensive IEP. (A selection of these elements are shown in the Appendix.)

The Individual Learning Programme (ILP) is only a part of the whole. Although we recognise that this model is not necessarily the standard model for an IEP and it may seem rather broad in nature, in order for pupils with PMLD to receive

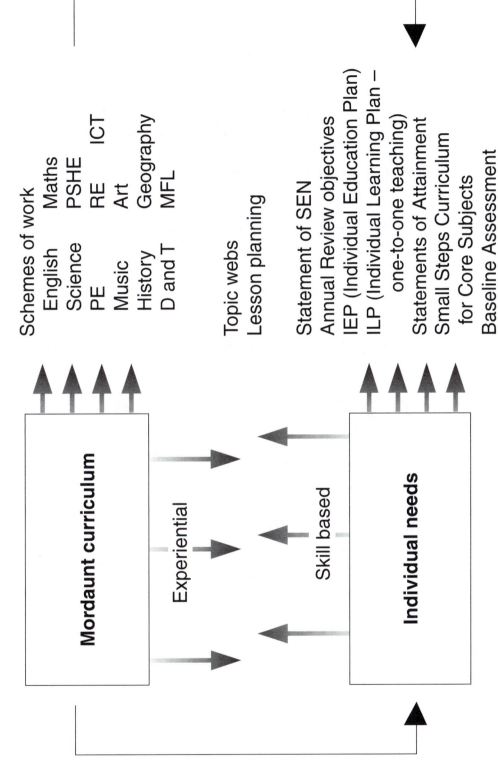

Breadth and balance shown between Mordaunt curriculum and individual needs of pupils

Schemes of work
English Maths PSHE
Science RE ICT
PE Art
Music Geography
History MFL
D and T

Topic webs
Lesson planning

Statement of SEN
Annual Review objectives
IEP (Individual Education Plan)
ILP (Individual Learning Plan – one-to-one teaching)
Statements of Attainment
Small Steps Curriculum for Core Subjects
Baseline Assessment

Mordaunt curriculum

Experiential

Skill based

Individual needs

Figure 1 Breadth and balance in the curriculum within the school day
© Mordaunt School, Southampton

19

Pupil information sheet

Annual review learning objectives*

Individual learning programmes (ILP)*

Moving and handling assessment*

Home/school physiotherapy management programme*

Occupational therapy objectives*

Speech and language therapy objectives*

Eating and drinking programme*

Enteral feeding programme*

Toileting programme and/or procedure

Individual timetable

Topic web

Daily activity sheets

Figure 2   Elements of an Individual Education Plan
© Mordaunt School, Southampton

the appropriate inclusive educational provision, which we believe is their right, account must be taken of every aspect of their needs. The resulting file becomes a vital working document that goes with the child throughout his or her time at the school and is available to all the professionals involved with child and family.

Having identified a need for a method of recording the small-steps learning objectives that were tailored to the individual needs of our students with PMLD, we know individual small step teaching is the most effective way for a pupil to achieve his or her skill-based learning objectives. These learning objectives must be relevant, realistic, achievable and measurable. The learning objectives that our pupils are working towards are most frequently found within the General Skills section of our curriculum. General skills are the building blocks of all subject areas and are the common denominator of every subject area of the National Curriculum. At the time of writing it is envisaged that our philosophy will be reflected by the QCA framework of P levels, 2000.

Individual learning programmes

Learning objectives are set at annual review and relate directly to Core Curriculum Records of Attainment. Prior to each child's annual review, meetings take place between all involved professionals so that the interdisciplinary process enables common goals to be set. Skill-based learning objectives are most frequently connected with communication which is part of the English curriculum and often accessed through information and communication technology by means of switches such as a Big Mack. These are long-term objectives from which the first small step is drawn. The teaching route towards these objectives will be unique to each child and at any point a learning step may have to be altered or an alternative route may be substituted in order to maintain progress. The ILPs are delivered on a daily basis. Therefore it is important to restrict the objectives to a manageable number – in our view a maximum of three should be used. Generalisation of the skills learned through ILPs will be discussed later in the book.

Developing our own documentation to record the skills learned through the ILPs involved reviewing existing documentation in use at other schools. This search showed a lack of appropriate material for our use. Therefore we devised our own ILP form (see Figure 3). It was important to include a clear visual and easily understood method of delivery in order to achieve a consistent way of working and recording because this is the evidence of progress and will inform the teacher of the next small step towards the long-term learning objective set at the annual review.

Teaching a learning objective through an individual learning programme

Delivering an ILP in our school involves a close intensive one-to-one session lasting five to ten minutes at most. The first step involves engaging the pupil by taking their lead, possibly using an intensive interaction approach (Nind and Hewett 1994). When the pupil is engaged, the programme can be carried out. It is important that for reasons of accuracy, recording takes place immediately. After ten sessions the programme is evaluated and the next step is identified. This next step may take the pupil forward, or targets may remain the same and be open to further evaluation after the next ten sessions. It may also mean taking a step back if the original step was inappropriate or circumstances such as the child's health needs prevented learning taking place or regression occurred (Male 2000; Brown 1996).

If a long-term objective has been achieved, it is necessary to return to the core curriculum statements of attainment to reassess and set an additional objective.

Explanation of completed Individual Learning Programme

Catherine is 10 years old and has Retts Syndrome. Over a number of years she has gained skills in the areas of English, IT and PE. She is now maintaining her skills in English and ICT but has regressed in her PE skills, i.e. she is no longer weight bearing.

This objective which was set at the annual review built on prior objectives for Catherine to choose an activity or toy by eye pointing, facial expression, whole-body movement and touch. She is able to initiate a request using the skills described above but this requires an adult to be working on a one-to-one basis. In the long term, to enable her to call attention to her needs and wants, we have introduced a switch. We will accept her present level of communication to express her choice of activity, but will use a full physical prompt (see Figure 3, shaded column 1) to press the switch which says 'I want that one'.

Individual Learning Programme

Record Sheet

Name	Catherine			Class 4		Term Spring 2000	
DOB	15 11 85			1 full physical prompt		4 verbal prompt	
Statement / Last Annual Review March 99				2 physical prompt		5 no prompt	
Curriculum area English		curr ref English GS Level D IT		3 gestural prompt		✓ comment	

Annual Review Objective

To communicate the desire for a toy to be activated or an action initiated

Start date	3 02 00	Date	1	2	3	4	5	Score ✓
Success criteria	3 attempts full physical prompt							
first small step								
Aim – Catherine to press a Big Mack switch to say 'I'd like to play that one' when asked which she wants to play with.		4/5	✓✓					3/3
Resources – See choice activities and preference assessment.		5/5	✓✓					3/3
Method – 1) Show 2 toys and name and play to encourage engagement between adult and child.		6/5	✓	✓✓				3/3
2) Stop at appropriate moment, ask Catherine which toy she would like showing each toy individually and naming – accept facial expression, eye pointing, whole-body movement.		7/5	✓✓	✓				3/3
		8/5	✓✓					3/3
3) Repeat her choice and allow Catherine 5–10 sec to initiate movement or help her to press Big Mack with full physical prompt.		11/5	✓	✓✓				3/3
		12/5		✓✓				3/3
4) Help Catherine to play with chosen toy.		13/5	✓	✓✓				3/3
5) Repeat twice more.		14/5	✓	✓✓				3/3

Evaluation 14/5   27/27   *Decrease prompt*
Date:

Figure 3   An example of a completed ILP record sheet
© Mordaunt School, Southampton

Individual Learning Programme

Record Sheet

Name Catherine	Class 4	Term Spring 2000
DOB 15 11 85	1 full physical prompt	4 verbal prompt
Statement / Last Annual Review March 99	2 physical prompt	5 no prompt
Curriculum area English	3 gestural prompt	✓ comment

Annual Review Objective: curr ref English GS Level D IT

To communicate the desire for a toy to be activated or an action initiated

Start date	3 02 00						
Success criteria	3 attempts full physical prompt						
first small step	Date	1	2	3	4	5	Score
	15/5	✓✓					0/5
	18/5	✓✓	✓				1/5
	19/5	✓	✓✓				2/5
	20/5		✓✓				3/5
	21/5	✓	✓✓				2/5
	22/5		✓✓				3/5
	25/5	✓	✓✓				2/5
	26/5		✓✓				3/5
	27/5		✓✓				3/5

Aim – Catherine to press a Big Mack switch to say 'I'd like to play that one' when asked which she wants to play with.

Resources – See choice activities and preference assessment.

Method – 1) Show 2 toys and name and play to encourage engagement between adult and child.
2) Stop at appropriate moment, ask Catherine which toy she would like showing each toy individually and naming – accept facial expression, eye pointing, whole-body movement.
3) Repeat her choice and allow Catherine 5–10 sec to initiate movement or help her to press Big Mack with full physical prompt.
4) Help Catherine to play with chosen toy.
5) Repeat twice more.

Continue as above

Evaluation Date: 27/6 $\frac{19}{27}$

Figure 3 An example of a completed ILP record sheet (continued)
© Mordaunt School, Southampton

We had previously determined Catherine's preferred activity or toy through a preference assessment.

Through intensive interactive approaches, combined with functional Communication, we have enabled Catherine to want to communicate with us and, more importantly, to see the benefits that communication brings her, so that we can build on this level of skill and move forward. For some pupils, we may be looking at the maintenance of these skills, for certain periods of their education. Catherine is also working on another objective in her second ILP. She needs to operate an adapted switch to activate a music programme on the computer with a full physical prompt (which is running concurrently) to help establish the switching skills in a different activity.

The next step in our example shows that the prompt was reduced to a physical prompt (see shaded column 2). The following step could be either to reduce the prompt to gestural or it might be to increase the time allowed for Catherine to initiate pressing of the switch. This decision will be made on the basis of the teacher knowing the pupil well enough to determine the way forward. This may not turn out to be the best way forward for this pupil at that time but, unless we try it, we will not know.

Records of Attainment/ core curriculum Statements of Attainment

The ILP objectives were taken from the Core Curriculum Statements of Attainment in maths, English and science which came from the Hampshire County Council *Working within Level One* documents. These documents were primarily curriculum documents which included statements of attainment and programmes of study. While these were a good starting point, we realised we would need to adapt them in order to be able to use them for skill-based assessment.

Because of the unique nature of the child with PMLD there is no assessment which will follow the child's own individual learning path but, as long as components of the earliest developmental levels are in place, the 'correct' order of these steps is not vital.

At the earliest level of development there is common ground or general skills across subjects. Therefore it is not necessary to have skill-based assessments in every subject. Rather they may be limited to maths, English and science to safeguard repetition as discussed earlier in the book when talking about P levels. In adapting the Hampshire document we used the statements of attainment with grading ranging from 'achieves occasionally' to 'achieves consistently' (see Figure 5).

We recognised that these steps are still often too broad but the skill and knowledge of the teacher of children with PMLD enables broad steps to be broken down into smaller steps through the planning of the ILP, which is unique to the individual child.

As we believe in an holistic approach to the education of our children, and since we have moved on from a purely skill-based form of teaching (whereby a child could not access the next step unless he or she had achieved the previous one), we needed to provide a much wider range of experiences. The introduction of the National Curriculum in mainstream settings provided the impetus to develop the Mordaunt School curriculum for pupils with PMLD.

Much discussion took place about the nature of learning by pupils with PMLD and the range of appropriate experiences. We came to the conclusion that our one-to-one teaching sessions (ILPs), where we focus mainly on communication skills, are an important but small part of our holistic philosophy. We felt our pupils needed a wider range of experiences which could be delivered through a specialised curriculum within group sessions, so that functional communication skills learned through the ILPs could be generalised. We believe these planned and focused group sessions provide progression of experiences by way of experiential learning opportunities which also give breadth and balance to the curriculum (Male 2000).

Mordaunt School curriculum

In order to develop our curriculum we looked at some of the curriculum documents already available. These helped to produce our maths, English, science, geography, history and ICT policy and curriculum documents. Additionally we used *Religious Education For All* (Brown 1996), *Music For All* (Wills and Peter 1996) and *Art for All* (Peter 1996) as references to help produce the RE, music and art policy and curriculum documents. The PE curriculum developed from integrating the therapy strands with our specialist knowledge of the physical needs of a child with PMLD.

Records of attainment **SCIENCE** **Name** ______________

KEY

●	╲	╳	■
achieves occasionally	achieves frequently	achieves consistently	reassess

General skills

Ea					React to sensory stimulation
Eb					Respond to sensory stimulation
Ec					Signal whether hungry or thirsty
Ed					Respond to clear bright colours
Ee					Show anticipation in familiar activities
Ef					Attend to held objects
Eg					Reach purposefully for an object
Eh					Cause movement in a variety of small objects
Da					Show interest in parts of their body
Db					Recognise main carers and familiar pupils
Dc					React consistently to stimuli which are liked/disliked

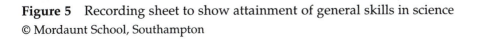

Figure 5 Recording sheet to show attainment of general skills in science

© Mordaunt School, Southampton

STATEMENT OF ATTAINMENT	EXAMPLES	LEARNING OPPORTUNITIES	RESOURCES
		PROGRAMMES OF STUDY	
		L E V E L C	
a) uses a variety of IT equipment and software including computers and various keyboards to carry out a variety of functions in a range of contexts	• reacts (by stilling, listening, looking, reaching, changing expression or posture, or vocalising) to devices being turned on and off; ranging from devices in a distraction-free environment to those in the community • responds (as above) to themed sensory rooms/areas and sensory drama activities • turns towards a burst of colour/light on a computer screen • attends to a variety of sounds on tape recorders • reacts to vibratory equipment • turns to the sounds of a supermarket checkout etc.	Pupils should be able to: • respond to a variety of IT equipment within the multi-sensory room and classroom • respond to use of computer systems and control opportunities in everyday life	computer/software touch screen concept keyboard tape recorders vibro-tubes - TFH vibro-beds - vibro-medico foot spas CCTVs television videos slides/projects interactive CDs CD rom supermarkets amusement arcades discos interactive museums shopping malls theme parks and funfairs turnstiles lifts escalators distraction free environment

Figure 6   A framework for the curriculum document
© Mordaunt School, Southampton

28

A curriculum needs to be relevant and must incorporate the good practice which is already taking place within a school. We found a useful framework for the curriculum document like the one in Figure 6 would include statements of attainment and programmes of study with examples of learning opportunities and suggested resources.

Within our curriculum there are many more examples than statements of attainment because we feel that they give the teachers more guidance in delivering group lessons.

Curriculum areas have been allocated to the teaching staff who are responsible for the relevant action plan, reviewing schemes of work, monitoring delivery of the subject and updating the policy and resources. A timetable for reviewing curriculum areas is identified within the School Development Plan and built into the forward planning schedule for staff meetings.

The curriculum as a whole is constantly being reviewed in line with national initiatives and, at the time of writing, we are in the process of a review in line with Curriculum 2000.

Schemes of work

In order to write our schemes of work we looked closely at the format of the curriculum initially in our core subject areas of maths, English and science and teased out those elements from the learning opportunities section that we felt could be part of our schemes of work. The remaining elements were those that we felt could best be taught through the ILPs because they were specific enough to be taught as part of a one-to-one teaching session if this was appropriate to the developmental level of a particular pupil.

As each of the remaining curricula was written, we followed the same process and this is ongoing. All the identified elements of a scheme of work were then allocated to each class after discussion between class teachers, to ensure that pupils were able to access the breadth and balance of the curriculum to which they are entitled. One element from each of the three schemes of work was recorded each term. When additional schemes of work were implemented, they too were recorded each term.

We recognised that although these elements were allocated to a defined class at a specific stage of the pupils' education, they could be repeated many times, such as in other group sessions, but they would only be formally recorded once.

Schemes of work and Records of Achievement and Experience

29

Scheme of work
SCIENCE

General skills

S1	level E	k/s 2	Contact and interact with staff and children within the whole school
S2	level E	Pre	Exploration of their scientific environment
S3	level E	Pre	Exposure to a variety of sensory stimuli both routine and occasional
S4	level E	k/s 1	Movement session in water
S5	level E	k/s 1	Relaxation and massage
S6	level E	k/s 4	Experience different weather conditions
S7	level E	k/s 1	Exposure to different light conditions
S8	level E	k/s 1	Push different objects to generate movement
S9	level E	k/s 3	Cause and effect relationships
S10	level E	Pre	Exposure to rhymes and simple songs
S11	level E	Pre	The exercise of choice
S12	level E	k/s 3	Practical problem solving
S13	level E	k/s 2	Name familiar objects
S14	level D	k/s 1	Watch objects being partially hidden and retrieved
S15	level D	k/s 3	One-to-one correspondence in everyday situations
S16	level D	k/s 2	Explore sequence in everyday life
S17	level D	k/s 3	Activate dangling object or computer programme
S18	level D	k/s 4	Explore the relationship between environmental clues and events

Scientific investigation – A.T. 1

S19	level C	Pre	Play with apparatus and toys worked by switches
S20	level C	k/s 4	Relate objects to their function
S21	level C	k/s 3	Experience movement of things in the natural world
S22	level B	Pre	Explore or experience a variety of sounds in play situations
S23	level B	k/s 4	Experience difference between still and moving water
S24	level B	k/s 2	Explore or experience a range of objects and substances

Life and living processes – A.T. 2

S25	level B	k/s 3	Respond to plants and animals with respect
S26	level B	k/s 4	Experience how we dispose of a range of waste products
S27	level A	k/s 4	Observe a variety of plants, using sight, touch and smell noting changes taking place during the seasons
S28	level A	k/s 4	Simple gardening
S29	level A	k/s 3	Simple food preparation

Materials and their properties – A.T. 3

S30	level C	k/s 1	Handle a range of different materials
S31	level A	Pre	Use flexible materials in a way that changes their shape

Physical processes – A.T. 4

S32	level C	k/s 2	Make sounds through musical instruments and our bodies
S33	level B	k/s 3	Play with light from different sources

Figure 7 Elements in a scheme of work for science

© Mordaunt School, Southampton

Once we had our schemes of work completed, we needed a method of delivering and recording them. More discussion amongst the whole school staff followed and we decided on delivery through group sessions, using a detailed lesson plan which showed the main aim of the lesson, often delivered through topic work.

Records of Achievement and Experience

When recording these schemes of work in our core subject areas of maths, English and science (and later PE), we acknowledged it was unlikely that there would ever be written evidence. Therefore we decided to use photographic records for our exemplification material as well as art work, and in some cases computer generated material. This recording formed the basis of a pupil's record of achievement (blank version shown in Figure 8A) as well as a teacher's recording sheet (Figure 8B).

We are aware that this form of recording is time consuming and very expensive so alternative methods of recording have been discussed. In religious education we use only a teacher-based recording sheet for each pupil (Figure 9).

Other schemes of work are yet to be fully developed.

Group teaching through experiential schemes of work gives opportunities for pupils to receive and respond to sensory stimuli, even though there may be no discernible progress in acquired knowledge or skills. However, we consider that experiential progress is as important to the pupils as skill-based progress.

Classroom organisation

The way in which the classroom is organised is an important factor in effective provision. Ware (1994) states that there are three components to classroom organisation. These elements are time, people and the material environment, all of which may overlap.

Time

Each class has a class timetable which enables all staff to know what is happening and for how long. It ensures breadth and balance over the school year. Each pupil has an individual timetable which largely follows the class timetable but allows for any variation such as music therapy sessions, riding for the disabled etc.

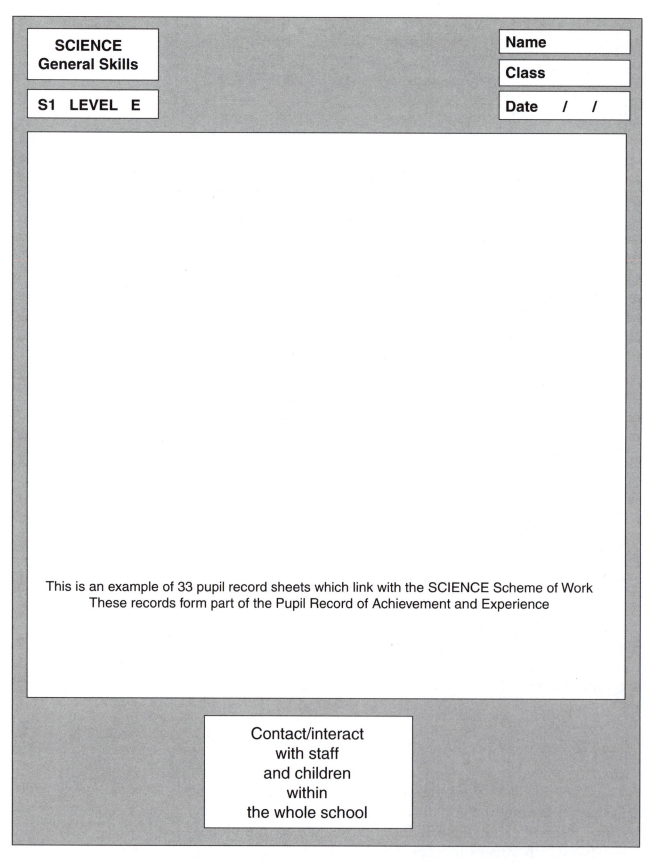

SCIENCE General Skills		Name
S1 LEVEL E		Class
		Date / /

This is an example of 33 pupil record sheets which link with the SCIENCE Scheme of Work
These records form part of the Pupil Record of Achievement and Experience

Contact/interact
with staff
and children
within
the whole school

Figure 8A   Recording achievement and experience linked to scheme of work (pupil record)
© Mordaunt School, Southampton

SCIENCE

Name _____

Records of Achievement and Experience

General skills			Date	Class	Teachers' comments	Signature

S1   LEVEL   E

Contact and interact with staff and children within the whole school   ___/___/___   [k/s **2**] [class]

S2   LEVEL   E

Exploration of their scientific environment   ___/___/___   [k/s **pre**] [class]

S3   LEVEL   E

Exposure to a variety of sensory stimuli both routine and elaborated   ___/___/___   [k/s **pre**] [class]

S4   LEVEL   E

Movement session in water   ___/___/___   [k/s **1**] [class]

S5   LEVEL   E

Relaxation and massage   ___/___/___   [k/s **2**] [class]

S6   LEVEL   E

Experience different weather conditions   ___/___/___   [k/s **4**] [class]

Figure 8B   Recording achievement and experience linked to scheme of work (teacher record)

© Mordaunt School, Southampton

R.E.

Name _____

Records of Achievement and Experience

AT 1   To have a knowledge and understanding of religious belief and practice

	Date	Key stage	Class		Comments

RE1

To be aware of the roles of special people within a personal and religious context

___/___/___   k/s **pre**   class

RE2

To be aware of special books and sacred writings

___/___/___   k/s **2**   class

RE3

To be aware that different religions have their own special buildings and places of worship

___/___/___

RE4   a)

To particpate in festivals and celebrations and to have a knowledge of signs, symbols and language within a religious culture:

	Date	k/s	class
A major festival or celebration	___/___/___	**pre**	
Shrove Tuesday	___/___/___	**1** a	
Holi	___/___/___	**2** a	
Easter	___/___/___	**3** a	b)
A Sikh festival	___/___/___	**4** a	
Divali	___/___/___	**1** b	
Harvest	___/___/___	**2** b	
A Jewish festival	___/___/___	**3** b	
Christmas	___/___/___	**4** b	

Figure 9   Record of achievement and experience limited to scheme of work: teacher-based recording sheet for religious education
© Mordaunt School, Southampton

A daily activity sheet is also used as a checklist to monitor whether the pupil's individual schedule is being followed. This form of recording is useful in identifying any parts of the timetable that are not being delivered. It is not about recording pupil progress, but about how time is managed. A class timetable cannot stand alone as it needs to link with the timetables of the nursing staff, the physiotherapists, the occupational therapists, the speech and language therapists and events such as orthotic clinics, wheelchair repairs, medical clinics, feeding clinics, annual reviews etc.

People

Each class has a teacher and two special school assistants (SSAs). The teacher has the overall responsibility for the organisation and deployment of staff within the classroom. Each SSA is allocated to work with specific pupils either on a one-to-one basis for ILPs, or a small group within a group lesson. At any given time there may also be therapists, nurses, students and volunteers within a class, all of whom may need direction and/or supervision by the teacher.

Material environment

As well as organising all necessary resources for the day, such as ICT equipment, and ensuring that equipment is available and in working order, it is important to be aware of all the aids that will be needed throughout the day such as:

- prone standers
- supine standers
- specialist walkers
- specialist seating
- body braces
- ankle foot orthoses
- dorsi-ankle foot orthoses
- hand splints
- leg gaiters.

Interdisciplinary liaison is essential to achieve a balance between the educational and therapy needs of the child but the overall responsibility for organising time, people and materials is that of the teacher.

Group lessons

Over a period of time, much discussion has taken place about the purpose of group lessons. We wrote our *Criteria for Planning a Lesson* (see Appendix, Section 5) because we felt we needed to make it plain that a group lesson is a combination of generalising the functional communication skills learned in a one-to-one teaching session (ILP) within a group context and giving experiential learning opportunities in a planned and focused way. Group teaching is not about sitting with an assessment chart ticking off a multitude of pre-planned objectives or writing reams of observations on each child after the lesson.

Because children with PMLD are operating at the earliest level of development, these functional communication skills are based within the general skills area of our whole core curriculum, irrespective of the subject focus. By generalisation it is important to ensure that pupils who have achieved a learning objective are given opportunities within a group lesson to use these skills. It is possible to give some time to allow responses allied to emerging skills presently being taught through an ILP, but these should not distract from the pace and focus of the lesson.

As there is generalisation of previously learned skills within each group lesson, there is no need for additional recording of information since it has previously been recorded within the pupil's ILP. Achievements which are outstanding or which demonstrate a skill that has not previously been observed are acknowledged in the lesson through verbal praise and are recorded through presentation of a Certificate of Achievement. Any skills that are consistently demonstrated within a group session may inform future planning of ILPs and may require a review of the records of attainment. Encouraging the generalisation of a skill and the recognition of emerging skills must be the responsibility of all staff participating in the lesson.

Initial assessment (This is Me)

When a child is admitted to the Early Years class it is important for the teacher to have knowledge of the whole child, e.g. seating, eating, drinking, aids, method of communication, likes, dislikes. Initially this information needs to be collected from all relevant professionals and collated by the teacher. In other schools this often happens after the child has been admitted. We did not feel this was satisfactory. Therefore the Early Years teacher decided this process must begin before the child starts school in order to build up effective home/school links, using the knowledge of the parents/carers as advocated in the Code of Practice (DfE 1994) and Home School Agreements (DfEE 1998). The teacher devised a *This is Me* record of achievement (Figure 10), based on a format used by some Portage groups for the initial assessment (see Bedford Portage Group 1994).

Baseline assessment

We did not want a framework that was imposed upon us which might not be entirely appropriate to our students. We believe that the baseline assessment helps to identify a pupil's developmental level and enables the teacher to prioritise areas for developmental target setting of small-steps skill-based learning objectives.

The headings within the baseline assessment recording sheet shown in Figure 11 are taken from the *Desirable Outcomes* (SCAA 1996a) and also relate to the latest *Early Learning Goals* (SCAA 2000) but are relevant to our pupils. We have used the same method of recording as in the core curriculum records of attainment, showing grading which ranges from 'achieves occasionally' to 'achieves consistently'. This baseline assessment has the added value of linking directly with core curriculum records of attainment throughout the pupil's time at school. Furthermore, within BATS, cross references enables the teacher to transfer knowledge of the child's developmental level identified in a baseline snapshot, to the core curriculum records of attainment. It is vital that a baseline assessment has the facility to link with a pupil's ongoing and future assessments. This will ensure there is continuity and meaning to future target setting.

Conclusion

During the writing of this book the authors have described the process they followed in developing the Mordaunt School Curriculum and the Baseline Assessment and Target Setting document. It is an ongoing process that is constantly changing and adapting to the needs of our pupils, whilst taking account of all new local and national initiatives. As practitioners we have tried to integrate the use of 'standardised' assessment materials with a more child-centred approach. Our pupils are at such an early developmental level that they need this holistic environment in order to maximise their learning.

All about me

My birthday is ☞ ----------------------------------

At home we speak ☞ ----------------------------------

When I play at home I use my

right hand ☐   left hand ☐   unsure yet ☐

Figure 10 Building up knowledge of the whole child with a This is Me record
© Mordaunt School, Southampton

Baseline Assessment

LANGUAGE AND COMMUNICATION

Name ....

KEY | **1** not at all | **2** occasionally | **3** frequently | **4** consistently

Does the child:	DATE				COMMENTS
1 show some intent to communicate e.g. indicate a need – continue/stop an activity					
2 attend to people in some way e.g. vocalise/change facial expression					
3 begin to show some consistency in response to adult interaction e.g. consistent vocalisation/gesture, giggles/to tickle etc.					
4 participate in turn-taking activities e.g. shaking/rattling tambourine etc.					
5 show understanding of: • gesture • objects of reference • pictures and photographs • signing • symbols • single words					
6 show some means of communicating by: • gesture • objects of reference • pictures and photographs • signing • symbols • single words					

Figure 11 Recording sheet for baseline assessment
© Mordaunt School, Southampton

39

One of the major issues facing us as practitioners in a school for pupils with PMLD is the issue of target setting for whole school improvement, as well as target setting to show individual progress. We have already discussed our belief that progression should be measured through both small-steps skill-based learning and through experiential learning opportunities. The school staff are now in the process of developing a system that will show progression by means of achieving an agreed percentage of our ILP targets linked to the School Improvement Plan. However, we also need to consider how targets which show whole-school progression in experiential learning opportunities can be developed.

In addition, we see the need for an even closer partnership between education, social services and health care professionals. This partnership will assume prominence as more and more profoundly disabled children with greater medical and social needs enter schools. At Mordaunt School we have been developing this partnership between all agencies and will continue to do so.

We are also aware that inclusion is one of the initiatives that will affect all special schools and we are concerned that the expertise and the specialism of the practitioners within a PMLD setting may be diluted. There is a real danger that the close working relationship between all agencies might not develop. We need to bear in mind that inclusion is not only about pupils with special needs being moved into mainstream schools but can also be inclusion within the local community while receiving education within a specialist setting.

Appendix

The appendix contains a selection of the contents of the Mordaunt School's BATS document which will support individual teachers and schools in their planning. These may be photocopied by the school or individual who purchased this book but after that all rights are reserved. See the biblio page or contact the publishers for further information.

Complete content of the Mordaunt School's BATS document

Section 1   **This is Me** (initial assessment)
             Baseline assessment
             Baseline and Records of Attainment cross reference

Section 2   **Records of Attainment**

- **English**   Record of Attainment

- **Maths**   Record of Attainment

- **Science**   Record of Attainment

- **PSHE**   Record of Attainment

Section 3   **Individual target setting**

- **Individual Learning Programme**

Section 4   **Schemes of Work and Records of Achievement**

- **English**   Scheme of Work
                Record of Achievement – teacher and pupil records
                Monitoring Sheets

- **Maths**   Scheme of Work
                Record of Achievement – teacher and pupil records
                Monitoring Sheets

- **Science**   Scheme of Work
                Record of Achievement – teacher's record
                Monitoring Sheets

© Mordaunt School, Southampton

- **IT**   Scheme of Work
             Record of Achievement – teacher's record
             Monitoring Sheets

- **RE**   Scheme of Work
             Record of Achievement – teacher's record
             Monitoring Sheets

- **PE**   Scheme of Work
             Record of Achievement – teacher's record
             Monitoring Sheets

- **Art**   Scheme of Work
             Record of Achievement – teacher's record
             Monitoring Sheets

Section **5**   **Forward planning: criteria for planning and evaluating a lesson**

- **Lesson Plan**

- **Criteria for planning a lesson**

- **Timetable**

- **Certificate of Achievement**

Section **6**   **Supplementary materials**

- **Curriculum diagrams and curriculum maps**

- **Individual eating and drinking programme**

- **Individual pupil moving and handling programme**

- **Individual enteral feeding programme**

- **Individual epilepsy protocol**

- **Individual medication protocol**

Selected extracts from the Mordaunt School's BATS document are provided in the following pages.

'This is Me' initial assessment

Mordaunt School Assessment Scheme _____

The purpose of the initial assessment:

- To give essential information at the earliest developmental stages about children who have additional complex needs.

- To inform all staff who are working with these pupils about their needs.

- To become a permanent record for parents and carers.

Guidance and suggestions for the initial assessment:

- It should be undertaken for all Early Years pupils during a home visit.

- It should be carried out before Early Years pupils begin school.

- It should be undertaken by the Early Years teacher.

- A health professional or school nurse may accompany the teacher.

- It may be adapted for older pupils.

- Not all the sheets need to be used.

Things I do

Things I really like

Things I really dislike

My Health

It is important for you to know

(Specific medical problems e.g. asthma, etc).

If I have a fit

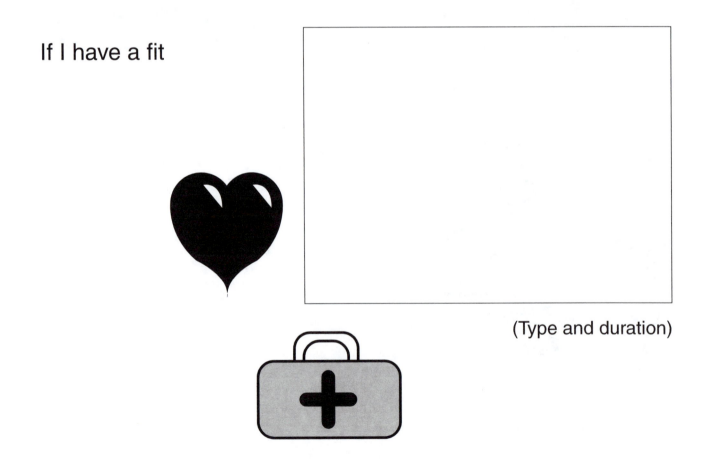

(Type and duration)

Records of Attainment

Mordaunt School Assessment Scheme _____

The purpose of the Records of Attainment:

- To provide a set of core curriculum statements.

- To show pupil progression from emergence of skills to skill consolidation.

- To be an ongoing record for the teacher.

- To show skill-based pupil progression, alongside experiential-based pupil progression (i.e. records of achievement and experience).

Guidance and suggestions for the Records of Attainment:

- Information from the baseline assessment to be transferred to the records of attainment by the first annual review of the statement.

- Objectives in the records of attainment should be linked with a pupil's annual review learning objectives.

- Pupils may have emerging skills in a number of the statements.

- Achieving an annual review learning objective does not necessarily mean that a pupil progresses to the following core curriculum statement. Pupils may need to continue work within the original core curriculum statement.

- The records of attainment should be updated annually.

- The records of attainment should be reviewed when a skill has been acquired.

Records of Attainment   **SCIENCE**   Name _____

General skills

Ea ☐ ☐ ☐ ☐   React to sensory stimulation

Eb ☐ ☐ ☐ ☐   Respond to sensory stimulation

Ec ☐ ☐ ☐ ☐   Signal whether hungry or thirsty

Ed ☐ ☐ ☐ ☐   Respond to clear bright colours

Ee ☐ ☐ ☐ ☐   Show anticipation in familiar activities

Ef ☐ ☐ ☐ ☐   Attend to held objects

Eg ☐ ☐ ☐ ☐   Reach purposefully for an object

Eh ☐ ☐ ☐ ☐   Cause movement in a variety of small objects

Da ☐ ☐ ☐ ☐   Show interest in parts of their body

Db ☐ ☐ ☐ ☐   Recognise main carers and familiar pupils

Dc ☐ ☐ ☐ ☐   React consistently to stimuli which are liked/disliked

© Mordaunt School, Southampton

Individual target setting

Mordaunt School Assessment Scheme _____

The purpose of individual target setting:

- To develop core skills that are appropriate to individual pupils.

Guidance and suggestions for individual target setting:

- An individual learning programme is a way of teaching targets through small-steps skill-based objectives.

- Targets should link with annual review objectives.

- Targets should be drawn from the records of attainment.

- Targets should be part of an ongoing assessment of pupils.

- Targets should be relevant, realistic, achievable and measurable.

- Targets should be generalised in group teaching.

- Targets should be delivered on a daily basis.

- No more than three skill-based targets should be delivered at any one time to ensure maximum learning.

Individual Learning Programme   **Record Sheet**

Name Catherine	Class 4	Term Spring 2000
DOB 15 11 85	1 full physical prompt	4 verbal prompt
Statement / Last Annual Review March 99	2 physical prompt	5 no prompt
Curriculum area English	3 gestural prompt	✓ comment
Annual Review Objective curr ref		

Start date		Date	1	2	3	4	5	Score	✓
Success criteria									
first small step									
Evaluation Date:									

Start date		Date	1	2	3	4	5	Score	✓
Success criteria									
first small step									
Evaluation Date:									

Section 4

Schemes of work and Records of Achievement and Experience

Mordaunt School Assessment Scheme _____

Schemes of work are:

- Drawn directly from the Mordaunt School PMLD curriculum.

- Recorded in the seven curriculum areas: English, maths, science, IT, RE, PE and art.

- Designed to ensure that pupils receive a broad and balanced experiential curriculum.

- Designed to incorporate the earliest developmental levels.

The purpose of the schemes of work:

- To draw experiences from the entire curriculum.
      (These experiences have not been written in a chronological series but can be used in any order.)

- To be a way of recording experiential progression.
      (i.e. the records of achievement and experience.)

- To show experiential-based progression, alongside skill-based pupil progression.
      (i.e. records of attainment.)

Guidance and suggestions for the schemes of work:

- Early years pupils are generally based at earlier developmental levels of the curriculum.

- Schemes of work can be delivered through group sessions.

Guidance and suggestions for the Records of Achievement and Experience:

- Record evidence of a broad and balanced experiential curriculum throughout pupils' time at school.

- Recording is completed through a teacher-based recording sheet.

- Records of achievement and experience in English, maths and science use a variety of exemplification materials (e.g. photos, art work etc.).

Note A set of monitoring sheets is included in this section.

© Mordaunt School, Southampton

Scheme of work
ENGLISH

General skills

E1	level E	pre	Developing an awareness of the environment
E2	level E	pre	Production of sound other than instinctive
E3	level E	pre	Exploration of and reaction to the immediate environment
E4	level D	pre	An exploration of objects
E5	level D	k/s 1	The association of cause and effect

Speaking and listening – AT 1

E6	level C	k/s 2	Developing a vocabulary of nouns and verbs
E7	level C	k/s 2	Developing attention and listening skills
E8	level C	k/s 1	Encouraging early imaginative play
E9	level C	k/s 4	Developing use of negatives and positives and simple concepts like big/little
E10	level B	k/s 3	Developing spatial awareness relating to people and objects
E11	level B	k/s 2	Listening skills in a group situation including anticipation and recall
E12	level B	k/s 1	Developing an understanding of the function of objects
E13	level B	k/s 2	Interactive play and early drama including role reversal and turn-taking
E14	level B	k/s 3	Using representational objects in an imaginative way
E15	level B	k/s 3	Developing understanding of basic concepts (e.g. clean/full/hot)
E16	level B	pre	Turn-taking with an adult
E17	level B	k/s 1	Simple rhymes

Reading – AT 2

E18	level A	k/s 1	Imaginative play and drama sessions including role play
E19	level C	k/s 4	Developing ideas of sequencing
E20	level C	k/s 4	Visual discrimination
E21	level B	k/s 4	Looking at books appropriately
E22	level B	k/s 3	Recognising signs and symbols (Makaton/Rebus/Everyday)

Writing, spelling and handwriting – AT 3 : 4 : 5

E23	level C	k/s 3	Developing hand/eye coordination

ENGLISH

Name _____

Records of Achievement and Experience

General skills		Date	Class	Teachers' comments	Signature

E1   LEVEL   E

Developing an awareness   ___/___/___ | k/s **pre** | class |
of the environment

E2   LEVEL   E

Production of sound   ___/___/___ | k/s **pre** | class |
other than instinctive

E3   LEVEL   E

Exploration of and   ___/___/___ | k/s **pre** | class |
reaction to the
immediate environment

E4   LEVEL   D

An exploration   ___/___/___ | k/s **pre** | class |
of objects

E5   LEVEL   D

The association of   ___/___/___ | k/s **1** | class |
cause and effect

Speaking and listening at 1		Date	Class	Teachers' comments	Signature

----

E6   LEVEL   C

Developing a vocabulary   ___/___/___ | k/s **2** | class |
of nouns and verbs

ENGLISH General skills	Name
	Class
E1 LEVEL E	Date / /

This is an example of 23 pupil record sheets which link with the ENGLISH Scheme of Work
These records form part of the Pupil Record of Achievement and Experience

Developing an awareness of the environment

ENGLISH

Scheme of work – individual pupil monitoring

General skills

E1 ☐ Developing an awareness of the environment

E2 ☐ Production of sound other than instinctive

E3 ☐ Exploration of and reaction to the immediate environment

E4 ☐ An exploration of objects

E5 ☐ The association of cause and effect

Speaking and listening

E6 ☐ Developing a vocabulary of nouns and verbs

E7 ☐ Developing attention and listening skills

E8 ☐ Encouraging early imaginative play

E9 ☐ Developing use of negatives and positives and simple concepts like big/little

E10 ☐ Developing spatial awareness relating to people and objects

E11 ☐ Listening skills in a group situation including anticipation and recall

E12 ☐ Developing an understanding of the function of objects

E13 ☐ Interactive play and early drama including role reversal and turn-taking

E14 ☐ Using representational objects in an imaginative way

E15 ☐ Developing understanding of basic concepts (e.g. clean/full/hot)

E16 ☐ Turn-taking with an adult

E17 ☐ Simple rhymes

Reading

E18 ☐ Imaginative play and drama sessions including role play

E19 ☐ Developing ideas of sequencing

E20 ☐ Visual discrimination

E21 ☐ Looking at books appropriately

E22 ☐ Recognising signs and symbols (Makaton/Rebus/Everyday)

Writing, spelling and handwriting

E23 ☐ Developing hand/eye coordination

Forward planning: Criteria for planning and evaluating a lesson

Mordaunt School Assessment Scheme _____

The following criteria were agreed when writing a lesson plan.

1   **Selecting individual teaching priorities**
    Generalisation of individual learning programme objectives is the aim.

    By generalisation we mean that it is important to ensure that pupils who have achieved or who are working towards an objective are given opportunities in a group session to use this skill.

    • This may require pupils to be prompted at a level lower than the current ILP prompt.

    • As this information is recorded in the pupils' ILP, basic generalisation of skills will not be recorded again.

    • Achievements which are outstanding or which demonstrate a skill that may not have been previously recorded will be acknowledged in the lesson through verbal and other praise and will be recorded through presentation of a certificate of achievement.

    • Any skills that are consistently demonstrated within a group session may inform future planning of ILPs and may require a review of the records of attainment.

    • Responsibility for encouraging the generalisation of a skill and the acknowledgement of this skill must be the responsibility of all staff who are part of the session.

    • Reinforcement of skills that have been previously learned should be practised.

2 Organisation of group lessons
Lessons will fall into a number of different categories:

A **Different programmes**	**Different curriculum areas** intrasequential teaching i.e. no systematic structuring of interaction
B **Different programmes**	**Same curriculum areas** intersequential structures i.e. some interaction between members of the group
C **Same programmes**	**Same curriculum areas** planned interaction i.e. more likely to bring about work as a group
D **Jigsawing**	a group activity is broken down into smaller components and each child or group of children is assigned a set of tasks.

• ILP lesson	**A**
• Whole class lesson	**B**
• Swimming	**B**
• Integrated English	**C**
• Integrated art	**C**

(Based on unpublished conference material by Porter and Lacey 1997.)

3 Content of lessons

This will either be the delivering of an individual learning programme or pupils will be experiencing a curriculum subject providing learning opportunities from the Mordaunt curriculum (see no 1 above).

4 Resources

These need to be planned in advance.
These need to be prepared in advance.
These need to be appropriate to the individual needs of the pupil.

5 Elements of a lesson

- <u>Structure</u> – beginning, middle, ending
  Use of objects of reference and symbols before each lesson.
  Inform class what is the content/purpose of lesson.
  Draw lesson to a close – reflect on what has been done/made.
  Ensure that there is an end of lesson 'reference'.

- **<u>Collaboration – use of assistants</u>**

- **<u>Balance of Activities</u>**

- **<u>Timing</u>**

- **<u>Duration</u>**

6   **Teaching style and pace**

It is recognised that children learn in different ways and that a range of teaching techniques will be used. Teaching methods adopted will be appropriate to individual needs and will take account of the curriculum or subject areas being taught.

7   **Seating and organisation**

Careful consideration needs to be given to the seating and organisation of the room bearing in mind staff support, resources and equipment available.

These needs can be met through class plans showing who is sitting where, how a pupil is sitting, and taking into account any equipment or additional considerations such as body belts, cushions etc. Correct positioning will therefore be part of the whole lesson and timing requirements will be made according to individual; and social requirements.

The pace of the lesson will depend on the type of lesson delivered and whether it is a whole group or individual lesson.

Lesson plan   Main aim:

Term		**Main curriculum focus**
Year	**Lesson**	**Additional curriculum areas**
Group		
Plan		**Curriculum references**
		More ideas / resources

Supplementary materials

Eating and drinking programme

Name		Class	DOB
Date		Review date	
Aim			

Position of feeder and child		Food texture and preferences and ALLERGIES	
Drinking method: Cup		Utensils	
Environment		Presentation of food	
Other requirements		Communication	
Teacher's signature		SALT signature		OT signature	

cc   parents   teacher   SaLT   OT   physio   medical officer   dietician   respite   other

Moving and handling assessment

Name						DOB	
Weight						Age	
Body shape	Tall		Medium height		Overweight		
	Short		Average weight		Underweight		

Disability	Ability to understand
	Any other problems
	Behavioural factors
Handling constraints	
Pain	
	Equipment used by child
Skin integrity	
Other	**Environment – risk factor**
Number of assistants required	
Teacher's signature	**Physiotherapist's signature**

Activities	Assistance required	Name
Walking		
Standing transfer		
Transfer to and from bed/chair		
Transfer to and from floor		
Transport to school		
Hydrotherapy		
Multi-sensory		
Horse riding		
Toileting		
Bathing		
Position and movement in bed		

Enteral feeding programme

Name		Class	
Date		Review date	

Aim

Route

Method (i.e. bolus or pump)

Type of feed

Time and quantity of feed

Oral feeding

Additional information

Size and make of tube

Other equipment

Teacher's signature		Nurse's signature	

References

Aitken, S. and Buultjens, M. (1992) *Vision for Doing*. Edinburgh: Moray House Publications.

Avon, Consortium of Teachers from the County of (1997) *Accreditation for Life and Living Skills*. OCR: Oxford, Cambridge and RSA Examinations Publications.

Bedford Portage Group (1994 – unpublished) *Assessment and Management of Children with Multiple Handicaps*. Bedford: Bedford Portage Group.

Brown, E. (1996) *Religious Education For All*. London: David Fulton Publishers.

Byrom, B. (1999) *Early Steps Summative Assessment*. B Squared.

Cunningham, C. E. *et al.* (1981) 'Behavioural and Linguistic Development in the Interactions of Normal and Retarded Children with their Mothers'. *Child Development*, **52**, 62–70.

Department for Education (1994) *The Code of Practice on the Identification and Assessment of Special Educational Needs*. London: HMSO.

Department for Education and Employment (1997) *Excellence for All Children: Meeting Special Educational Needs*. London: HMSO.

Department for Education and Employment (1998a) *Home School Agreements, Guidance for Schools*. London: DfEE.

Department for Education and Employment (1998b) *Meeting Special Educational Needs – A Programme For Action*. London: DfEE.

Department for Education and Science (1944) *Education Act*. London: HMSO.

Department for Education and Science (1970) *Education (Handicapped Children's) Act*. London: HMSO.

Department of Education and Science (1978) *Special Educational Needs: Report of the Committee of Enquiry into the Education of Handicapped Children and Young People (The Warnock Report)*. London: HMSO.

Department for Education and Science (1981) *Education Act*. London: HMSO.

Department for Education and Science (1988) *Education Reform Act*. London: HMSO.

Department for Education and Science (1989) *The Children Act*. London: HMSO.

Department for Education and Science (1993) *Education (Schools) Act*. London: HMSO.

Goldbart, J. (1994) 'Opening the Communication Curriculum for Students with PMLD'. In Ware, J. (ed.), *Creating a Responsive Environment*. London: David Fulton Publishers.

Hampshire County Council (1993) *Working Within Level One of the National Curriculum*. Hampshire: unpublished.

Hanzlik, J. R. (1990) 'Non-verbal Interaction Patterns of Mothers and their Infants with Cerebral Palsy. Educating and Training'. *Mental Retardation* **25**(4),333–4.

Houghton, J. *et al.* (1987) 'Opportunities to Express Preferences and Make Choices among Students with Severe Disabilities in Classroom Settings'. *Journal of the Association for Persons with Severe Handicaps* **12**, 18–27.

Kent Curriculum Services Agency (1995) *Crossing the Bridge*. Canterbury: South East Information Network.

Kent Curriculum Services Agency (1996) *Crossing the Bridge (II)*. Kent: Kent County Council.

Kiernan, C. and Jones, M. C. (1982) *Behaviour Assessment Battery*. Windsor: NFER/Nelson.

Kiernan, C. and Reid, B. (1986) *Pre-Verbal Communication Schedule*. Windsor: NFER/Nelson.

Male, D. (2000) 'Target Setting in Schools for Children with Severe Learning Difficulties: Headteachers' Perceptions'. *The British Journal of Special Education* **27**, 6–12.

Nind, M. and Hewett, D. (1994) *Access to Communication: Developing the Basics of Communication with People with Severe Learning Difficulties Through Intensive Interaction*. London: David Fulton Publishers.

Northern Ireland Curriculum Council (1991) *Stepping Stones*. Belfast: NICC.

Ouvry, C. (1987) *Educating Children with Profound Handicaps*. Kidderminster: BIMH.

Peter, M. (1996) *Art for All (II)*. London: David Fulton Publishers.

Porter, J. and Lacey, P. (1997) Meeting the Needs of Individual Pupils with Severe Learning Difficulties in Group Settings. Unpublished Conference Material from The Hampshire Curriculum Conference: Marwell.

Qualification and Curriculum Authority (1998) *Supporting the Target Setting Process*. London: QCA Publications.

Qualification and Curriculum Authority and DfEE (1999) *The National Curriculum Handbook for Primary Teachers in England*. London: HMSO.

Qualification and Curriculum Authority (2000) *Investing in Our Future: Curriculum Guidance for the Foundation Stage*. London: QCA Publications.

Schools Curriculum and Assessment Authority (1996a) *Desirable Outcomes for Children's Learning on Entering Compulsory Education*. London: SCAA Publications.

Schools Curriculum and Assessment Authority (1996b) *Planning the Curriculum for Pupils with Profound and Multiple Learning Difficulties*. London: SCAA Publications.

Schools Curriculum and Assessment Authority (2000) *Early Learning Goals: Curriculum Guidance for Foundation Stage*. London: SCAA Publications.

Scoville, R. (1984) Development of the Intention to Communicate: The Eye of the Beholder. In Fagens, L., Garvey, C. and Golinkoff, I. R. (eds) *The Origins and Growth of Communication*. NJ: Ablex Publishing Corporation.

Sebba, J. *et al.* (eds) (1993) *Redefining the Curriculum for Pupils with Learning Difficulties*. London: David Fulton Publishers.

Simon, G. B. (1986) *The Next Step on the Ladder Development Assessment Scale*. Kidderminster: BIMH Publications.

Teacher Training Agency (1998) *National Standards for Special Educational Needs (SEN) Specialist Teachers*. London: TTA.

Terdal, L.E. *et al.* (1976) Mother-Child Interaction: A Comparison Between Normal and Developmental Delayed Groups. In Mash, E. J., Hamerlynck, L. A. and Handy, L.(eds) *Behaviour Modification and Families*. New York: Brunner/Mazel.

Uzgiris, I. C., and Hunt, J. McV (1975) *Assessment in Infancy: Ordinal Scales of Psychological Development*. Illinois: Urbana University.

Ware, J. and Healey, I. (1994) Conceptualising Progress in Children with Profound and Multiple Learning Difficulties. In Ware, J. (1994) *Educating Children with Profound and Multiple Learning Difficulties*. London: David Fulton Publishers.

Ware, J. (1994) Classroom Organisation. In Ware, J. (1994) *Educating Children with Profound and Multiple Learning Difficulties*. London: David Fulton Publishers.

Ware, J. (1996) *Creating a Responsive Environment*. London: David Fulton Publishers.

Wills, P. and Peter, M. (1996) *Music For All*. London: David Fulton Publishers.

Wolfendale, S. (1993) *Assessing Special Educational Needs*. London: Cassell.

Index